Zen for Beginners

Your Guide to Achieving Happiness and Finding Inner Peace with Zen in Your Everyday Life

Susan Mori

There are no scenarios in which the publisher or the original author of this work can be, in any fashion, deemed liable for any hardship or damages that may befall them after undertaking information described herein.

Additionally, the information in the following pages is intended only for informational purposes and should thus be thought of as universal. As befitting its nature, it is presented without assurance regarding its prolonged validity or interim quality. Trademarks are mentioned without written consent and can in no way be considered an endorsement from the trademark holder.

Table of Contents

Introduction

Congratulations on buying the paperback version of *"Zen for Beginners: Your Guide to Achieving Happiness and Finding Inner Peace With Zen in Your Everyday Life "* and really thank you for doing so.

The following chapters will discuss Zen philosophy and how you can apply it to your everyday life, relationships, work, and finances, as well as how it will benefit your health and happiness. Zen is a Buddhist belief system and a philosophy that can be learned by just about anyone.

In chapter one, you will learn about the history of Zen, why it is important, and the basics of following it. In chapter two, you will learn how to embody Zen daily, even in mundane situations, for a happier and more peaceful life. In chapters three through five, you will learn about applying Zen on your relationships, work, and finances to further improve those aspects of your life. Chapter six will cover how Zen works and how it can benefit your health and happiness.

By including Zen in your day-to-day life you will

enjoy benefits like reduced stress, stronger relationships, a decluttered mind and home, wisely managing your money, a more open and understanding outlook, a more enjoyable work life and stable career, peace of mind, better health, and more. By implementing even a few of the simple changes discussed in this book, you can start making improvements to your life.

There are plenty of books on this subject on the market, so thanks again for choosing this one! Every effort was made to ensure it is full of as much useful information as possible. Please enjoy!

<u>Chapter 1: What Is the Zen Philosophy?</u>

To understand how you can achieve happiness and find inner peace with Zen, you must first understand what it is. Zen is one type of Buddhist practice. Buddhism originated in India, near modern Nepal, in the sixth century, B.C. Buddhism was founded by a prince named Siddhartha Gautama. When he was twenty-nine, Siddhartha Gautama persuaded his parents to let him see the outside world, and as a result, he experienced what suffering truly meant for the first time. This led him on a path to understanding human suffering, its causes, and how to stop it.

To find the answer, Siddhartha Gautama meditated for forty-nine days straight, and through that trial, he became the first enlightened human, a Buddha. He then taught what he learned to the rest of India. From there, his teachings traveled to China, where Chinese culture influenced the philosophies.

Zen is one of the schools of Mahāyāna Buddhism that began during the reign of the *Tang* dynasty China (618–907). Today, *Mahāyāna* Buddhism is the largest surviving Buddhist tradition. In the

Mahāyāna tradition, the *Bodhisattva*, (those who attain Buddhahood through the path to enlightenment) aid others on their path to enlightenment. By gaining the aid of the *Bodhisattva*, enlightenment can be achieved in one lifetime, which is not taught in other Buddhist traditions where the focus is on karma and reincarnation.

Zen was profoundly influenced by Taoism (also known as Daoism). Taoism is both a religious and philosophical tradition that also originated in China. Taoism can be translated as 'the way' and puts emphasis on taking action without intention (*wu wei*). 'Action without intention' is a belief that has a sort of inherent naturalness that involves living simply and spontaneously. Another essential aspect of Taoism are the three tenets of compassion, frugality, and humility. These concepts are profoundly ingrained in Zen.

From China, this new form of Buddhism traveled to the rest of Asia including Vietnam, Korea, and Japan. It was in Japan that it gained its most popular name, Zen, because of the Japanese pronunciation of the Middle Chinese word *Chan* which has meaning in meditation. From Japan, Zen traveled worldwide. It became especially popular in the sixties because of its emphasis on attaining a higher state of mind through relaxation, living simply, and compassion, all commonly seen in the Hippie subculture popular at the time in the United States.

Although Zen is a school of Buddhism, and thus a religion, it is also a philosophy, and as such you do not need to quit any existing religion or ascribe to becoming a Buddhist to practice it. The core aspects of Zen, which will be described in detail in the following pages, can be easily applied to fit many situations and are practiced by nonreligious people and religious people of many faiths worldwide.

Overall, Zen is a practice of achieving self-control and insight through meditation. This is done through observing one's breath, observing the mind, several types of meditation, and sometimes, chanting sutras. Observing the breath is a process of regulating the mind by becoming aware of your breaths and the energy they bring through the center of the body, the area right below the navel. Observing the mind is a method of letting your thoughts flow without interfering or lingering on them. Chanting sutras is a practice in many monasteries and liturgy services and can be used as a means to connect with the *Bodhisattvas*.

Also, Zen Buddhism has many other religious

aspects such as public services, weddings, and funerals.

Introduction to Zen teachings

Although Buddhism does not have a strong doctrinal history, there are still plenty of teachings that have been passed down through the centuries. In fact, there are so many teachings and different schools that it is nearly impossible to narrow down the entirety of Zen Buddhism to a few select lessons.

However, the few things that are common to all Zen schools of teaching are accepting reality as it is, striving for a Buddha-like nature, the goal of becoming a *Bodhisattva*, and the necessity of meditation. Zen teachings can be thought of as directions one can follow to achieve a higher level of awakening. They point towards a deeper understanding while simultaneously telling you that the teachings themselves are not the only form of understanding you should be striving for. Zen teachings are merely a tool that people can use to find their own truths.

There are two ways for people to understand Zen. In Chinese, these ways are called *pen chueh* and *Shih-chueh*. *Pen Chueh* says that human minds are fully enlightened from the beginning while *Shih-chueh* says that human minds are ignorant and each individual experiences a point of awakening to becoming enlightened.

Two schools of Zen found in Japan are *Rinzai* and *Soto*. *Rinzai* descended from the Chinese school *Linji* and put importance in finding one's true nature, known as *kensho*, and practices it to attain Buddhahood. In this school, both meditation (*zazen*) and simultaneous study of scripture (*kōan*) are especially important. *Rinzai* practitioners can focus on a *kōan* while meditating to keep their mind free. *Soto* descended from the Chinese school *Caodong*, unlike *Rinzai*, this school does not focus on *kōan* study, but rather *shikantaza*, a different form of meditation in which an individual focuses on suspending judgment and giving their thoughts free rein. This form of meditation is often referred to as 'just sitting' and is the most practiced technique among people who have not ascribed to becoming a Buddhist.

As for Zen scripture, contrary to common belief, it is not usually crucial in Zen teachings. Zen monks are expected to know the history and common themes of their beliefs and Zen masters are quite knowledgeable on *Mahāyāna* sutras, but the average student does not need to learn, let alone, memorize Zen scripture.

Zen emphasizes conceptualization rather than insight through study. As such, it is vital that one should be introspective and develop a greater understanding of other people instead of focusing on intellectual study. There are even terms for people who only pursued intellectual understanding without practicing Zen; they are called *yako-zen* or 'wild for Zen' and *zen temma* or 'Zen devil.'

Despite how unimportant the scriptures are in learning Zen, to legitimize the practice and separation as an individual school of Buddhism early on in China, many scriptures were written, and a significant amount of literature is still available. These include the *Śrīmālādevī* Sutra, the *Lankavatara* Sutra, the 'Platform' Sutra, the *Vimalakirti* Sutra, and many more.

Throughout history, even with the changes in schools, and new literature, the Zen Philosophy stayed rooted in 'The Four Noble Truths' that were originally understood by Buddha after he gained enlightenment. These truths are:

- Life is suffering

- Suffering is caused by human desires

- Desires must be stopped

- To stop our desires, we must understand the 'Eightfold Path.'

Although the idea that life is only full of suffering is rather depressing, it is not meant to be so. It is meant to teach us how we can accept our suffering to move overcome it.

The second truth reveals why we suffer. It lies in our desire for things. Desire can easily and quickly lead us down a path of destruction just to obtain that what we want. If you can accept your suffering, then you can avoid suffering.

This leads to the third truth, giving up desire. Doing so does not have to mean a loss of love, emotions, or activities. It means letting go of things that you cannot have, and you should just let life bring everything you need. This can also be found in Taoism, which teaches us that inaction is the path to happiness.

The fourth truth is the means to ending the suffering caused by desire. It shows you the path which will lead to your goal, although the steps are not meant to be followed one by one but all at once. The 'Eightfold Path' is as follows:

- ***Right view***
  Become aware of the actions you make, the actions of others, and the motivations behind them and understand that nothing is permanent, including your idea of 'self.'

- **Right Intention**

  Become aware of your feelings of desire, judgment, and anger and resist acting on them. Be sure to only act if your intentions are motivated by doing good things for others, not just yourself.

- **Right speech**

  Keep in mind that words can harm other people, which is why you need to be careful with what you say. Do not lie, spread deceit, or speak harshly. Speak only if you have something nice to say or contribute.

- **Right action**

  Do not harm people, animals, or your surroundings. This includes murder, theft, and molestation above all else.

- **Right livelihood**

  This path means that one should live honestly by doing a job that will help others. Do not do something just to get rich or with the intention of harming. Avoid dealing with weapons, meat production, alcohol, or drugs and do not engage in a profession in which the goals are contrary to right speech and right action.

- **Right effort**

  Apply effort in making the correct actions

by not doing something that can hurt others and actively doing good things whenever possible.

- *Right mindfulness*

  This refers to being able to observe and understand yourself as well as focusing on the here and now around you. This also refers to refraining from making a quick judgment and incorrect interpretations.

- *Right concentration*

  This refers to meditation and achieving a greater level of understanding through a focused state of mind.

Introduction to meditation

Meditation is important to Zen because of the focus on mindfulness and understanding. Meditation is an exercise meant to give us peace of mind. To begin, choose a place and time where you will be free from distractions. It's better to do this in the morning which will prepare you for the day or the evening which will prepare you for a wonderful sleep. Choose one or both and create a routine. Do not switch between morning and evening.

Setting the alarm will help you keep track of time as having to watch the clock disrupts one's focus.

Next, find a comfortable position in which to meditate. You do not have to do a lotus position with your legs crossed and feet on your thighs. In fact, if that is not a comfortable position, avoid it completely. Sitting on the floor is not a requirement either, just sitting on a chair is fine. A lot of people find a cushion or mat to be the most comfortable. Choosing a position that you do not use often may help with focus, but only if it is comfortable enough to not become disruptive.

The half lotus position is what many practitioners prefer while meditating. To perform the half lotus, you just need to sit on the floor and cross your legs, bend your left leg, and rest the sole of your foot on the inside of your right leg, bend your right leg until you can put it on your left knee, and push your knees down as far as possible. Make sure that your back is straight, your shoulders are relaxed, and keep your eyes relaxed but not fully closed. Place your hands on your knees in a comfortable position.

As a beginner, your meditation sessions should last around five to ten minutes. As you become more experienced and used to the process, you can increase the time to about twenty to thirty minutes. Most people do not meditate longer than that.

The goal of Zen meditation is to experience and

analyze your senses and thoughts, not to daydream or enter a trance. Do not control your thoughts. Instead, let them flow through you without lingering too much on them.

To remain focused, observe your breaths to immerse yourself in the meditation. Breathe deeply from your stomach, count your breaths, and feel the sensation of breathing. Count as you inhale and exhale. Start over if you lose count, but do not get frustrated. Once you get the hang of meditation, you can stop counting and just focus on your breaths. As soon as your alarm goes off, take your time ending the session. Instead of jumping out of it right away, try to ease yourself out of it gently, so you'll feel the effects of meditation last for the rest of the day.

To live the Zen way, all you have to do is live the way you usually do, but with the addition of mindfulness. Zen will change your life naturally if you incorporate it. Understanding others and focusing on meditation will help you concentrate on each thing you do and enjoy life to the fullest. When you are with someone, you will focus on them entirely. When you work, you will work to your full potential. In return, the world you live in will become one with you, and you will become as calm and unmovable as a tree.

Chapter 2: How to Practice Zen in Your Everyday Life

Now that you have an understanding of what Zen is and what its practices are, you can learn how to apply it to your life. Simplicity, mindfulness, concentration, and calmness are all the principles of Zen that you should strive to learn even if you do not want to become a Zen monk. This chapter will explain some easy tips that anyone can follow to change your life for the better.

While you learn about these principles, keep in mind that the point is to bring the spirit of Zen into your life. You have the power of Zen within you, and all you have to do is bring it into the world alongside you. Even if you are a complete beginner to Zen and have never practiced it, it should still resonate with you as a good way to live.

It has even been theorized that if more people applied Zen to their lives many problems of the modern world would be solved.

Figuring out how to apply Zen in your everyday life may be difficult at first, and sometimes, the principles may be nearly impossible to apply, but any effort you put forth into Zen will ultimately be worth it in the end. You will see an improvement in your happiness and peacefulness in life along with your routines and outlooks. Imagine what you could get done by applying all of the advice provided in this book.

The following advice was created with the use of the 'Eightfold Path' you read about in chapter one. Each aspect is interconnected to the others. Some will be easier while some will be slower to apply to your life. On the whole, this is not about achieving perfection as that would be contrary to the spirit of Zen.

Give every action your full attention

This means doing one thing at a time, deliberately, with your full attention. If you will do something, understand the act in its entirety and do it with every fiber of your being. This can be applied to every action you do. A Zen proverb states: "When walking, walk. When eating, eat."

This can be applied to everything you do throughout the day. If this advice seems too difficult, it may mean that you need it the most. Divide your time equally so that you can fully devote yourself to one task at a time. If you will spend time with family, be mentally and physically present. If you have to clean, remain focused and motivated. Multitasking is not a part of Zen.

The second aspect of this is doing everything deliberately. This goes beyond only doing one thing at a time. Do not rush your tasks. Take time to focus and invest yourself in the things you do.

Also, you must do each thing completely. Make sure to put your entire self into your daily tasks and to remain focused until it is done. Even if you cannot complete a task in one try, be sure to put it away and clean up before moving on. This will allow you to give the other things you will do your full attention as well.

Also related to this principle is that you should do less while leaving time to spare between tasks. By focusing on what is important and dedicating yourself fully to each aspect of your life, you will do things better. By leaving space in your schedule, you will have time for something unexpected or if something takes longer than planned.

Form routines

Routines and rituals for completing tasks are key

to the Zen lifestyle. Routines naturally lead to a more peaceful mind because you will have less to think about or remember and have more time to enjoy the present. Removing the need for reminders throughout the day will free you from a lot of disorder and distraction. This does not have to be done so thoroughly that your entire life is scheduled, it just has to be your important daily and weekly activities. Anything that falls outside of what you consider an important activity can be kept in a list or calendar.

Besides your day, you should also be forming rituals for completing tasks. These mini-routines will help focus your attention, keep your pace, and help you understand what is important in your activities. Zen monks form a variety of rituals, but you can apply this skill to your own activities such as cleaning, work, and cooking.

These practices should help you not waste time, become more efficient, and liberate yourself from watching the clock. Besides that, being organized is good for the mind and body.

Dedicate time for meditation

Meditation is a very important aspect of practicing Zen, as explained in chapter one. You should devote some of your time to actual mediation every day. However, you can also bring aspects of meditation into your other activities and effectively blend it into your day. This is very effective for living in the modern world and will help you remain present at the moment. Meditating helps you concentrate on the here and now.

It is very important to make meditation a habit as well. Make sure that you do it every day. Try meditating while bathing, cooking, cleaning, or waiting. This is essentially taking the advice of giving every action your full attention to the next level by forcing you to remain focused on what you are doing at the moment, and this is also a great way to practice mindfulness.

Respect and appreciation for life

This includes respecting and appreciating your own life, the lives of others, the lives of animals, and how it is all connected. This should be a simple practice. Things like, not killing or harming plants or animals unless it is necessary, reducing waste, and aiding others when needed are included in this Zen practice, and many people do them every day. Take time to understand, respect, and find significance in your place in the natural world. You will be surprised by how much appreciating nature can help you in dealing with stress.

Simplify your life

This is both for activities and material possessions. Starting with your activities, it is important in Zen to remove what is cluttering your life by removing things that are unimportant. This should be applied to every aspect of your life.

Start by deciding what things are unessential or less important to you. What you deem as essential aspects of your life will be different for every individual. For someone, their hobbies and their family might be the most important aspects of their life. For another, it might be religion, friends, and their work. It is up to you to pick the things that mean the most. The goal is to remove as much as you can to make time for the essentials.

The same concept can be applied to material possessions. When you think of a Zen monk, they lead simple lives as much as possible. They only eat, walk, act, and live in the most basic ways. This is not necessary for the average person, but it should be kept as a reminder of how much of your life is truly not necessary in a way. Take extra things out of your home. Decide if you need every item you own. If the answer is yes, by all means, don't throw it out, but if the answer is no, maybe the best thing to do is to throw it away or donate it to someone who does need it.

Humans tend to hold on to things that are sentimental or because we think that it's more troublesome to get rid of it. A good example is the things you find at the bottom of your junk drawer. Those are things that you should think about not keeping. This being said, you certainly don't have to get rid of every item that makes you happy. However, even getting rid of a few unnecessary items will have a positive effect on your mental state and the cleanliness of your home.

It might also help if you limit your exposure to any outside influences. Television, relationships, social media, and news can have a profound effect on your mind and the ability to focus. The most difficult thing you might have to work on is your relationships because deciding whether or not to keep someone who is negative and willingly bringing you down is not easy.

Besides that, lessening how often you absorb outside media from the television, radio, or internet will help with clearing your mind. Try to replace your entertainment with positive books (fiction is okay), audio, television, environments, and people.

Reevaluate your goals

Almost everyone has a goal of some kind. The problem lies in becoming too attached to it and making your happiness in life dependent on accomplishing it. By reevaluating your goals, you can decide if that goal is truly worth your happiness, why you want to achieve it, if it is worth the amount of time it will take, and if it is self-serving or helpful to the world around you. If you find yourself saying that you will be happy once it happens, you might have placed too much importance on a singular goal. You do not have to give up your goals, but you need to focus on the happiness you can find in the present as well. You may discover that you have been missing multiple opportunities in pursuit of your happiness.

Overall, all of the Zen practices can be performed by everyone. The principles can be applied to anyone's life regardless of your beliefs, standards of living, or health.

Chapter 3: Applying Zen to Your Relationships

People will have many relationships in their lives, whether they are romantic or platonic. Applying Zen to your relationships can help you keep the peace and understand both yourself and other people.

One of the most important aspects of Zen that you can apply in every relationship is to refrain from making quick judgments. As you read in chapter one, this is related to the second of the 'Eightfold Paths.' This practice can save relationships.

The only thing that making judgments does is create fixed ideas about other people and your environment. Clinging to your biased notions can create strife between people. Always make sure that you are correct in your immediate perceptions before acting on them. For example, you might feel scared after seeing something in a dark room, but if you turn on the light, it's probably nothing. Always make sure to hold back on prematurely judging other people before acting on them.

Also, be sure to apply the third and fourth lessons

of the Eightfold Paths when you interact with other people. Making sure your speech and actions are kind and appropriate for the situation at hand is key. A good example is when you talk about someone. Avoid biased judgment by saying like "They said they would do that, but did not." Instead of "They are thoughtless," say, "I haven't been in touch with them for a while." Instead of "They are ignoring me," say, "They are busy with something right now, I'll come back later," instead of, "They don't want to spend time with me."

Remember, you do not know what is happening in other people's lives unless you talk to them about it. They might not be acting the way you expect, have hurt your feelings, or ignored you, but they probably have not done so on purpose. Your friend or partner might have problems with their other friends or family, have medical problems, be uncomfortable with your current issues, or they could just be busy. Recognize that everyone has a life as complicated as yours. Reaching out to them to have a talk can help you both understand each other. If it is time to end a relationship, at least you will both understand why. Before letting go someone because of your preconceived notion, make sure that judgment is correct.

One of the problems that can arise in a

relationship is that one person is not happy and has become dependent on the other person for happiness and validation. Insecurity and jealousy might develop. One person supplying all the needs in a relationship is not healthy as they will only deprive themselves of their freedom.

This is an issue that needs to be solved internally. Anyone can benefit from focusing on themselves even if you do not think this problem applies to you at the moment. An important aspect of Zen is learning how to understand yourself to help you become a person who is happy in your own skin and does not need validation others to feel secure. Accepting yourself and loving yourself will make a world of difference in your relationships.

Loving yourself and not needing other people to provide your happiness does not mean that you do not need love or other people in your life. It only means that you have provided the foundation to stay independent by loving yourself if other people fail to provide the love you're seeking.

By building up this foundation of self-love, you will feel more secure. You won't need to worry about your friends or partners leaving because even though it would be a loss, you would not lose yourself in the process. You will be fine just by yourself, and your self-esteem will be affected positively as well. You won't need constant reassurance of other people's love for you, and you will be able to trust them easier.

That being said, a good relationship is built by two people who feel secure and confident in themselves. They will not be in a relationship that is based on needs but on companionship. If only one person is secure, the burden on the other person is heavy and the relationship will be unhealthy and won't last long. Speak to the people you care about and make sure you help them feel whole as a person.

Remember that in any relationship, romantic or platonic, having too great of mutual neediness means that neither person will have freedom in their lives. Even the most loving relationships need some distance for the individuals to have other healthy friendly, familial, or romantic relationships as well as have time for themselves to spend on hobbies and rest.

If you feel the need to constantly check in on your friends, family, or partner, you should work on how you can feel happy about yourself. You should be able to part ways from people you hold dear and still know they care about you. Work on letting go of what makes you insecure. You're an amazing person all by yourself. You are good

that can hurt others, observe and understand yourself, and refrain from making quick judgments or incorrect interpretations. This boils down to not starting an argument without first understanding why you are angry and what the other person did to make you feel that anger.

Erotic relationships and Zen

Once you move past a romantic relationship into being intimate with another person, you have opened up new opportunities for friction. Sexual relationships are not often mentioned in Zen Buddhist teachings, but keeping a Zen mindset should help you keep a healthy and happy relationship no matter what kind it is.

Talking about sex is important to romantic relationships, especially since you will be doing it. We live in a society where it is shown and talked about often, but it is not often talked about positively in that media. Sex is also often unnecessarily linked to a person's self-esteem. Being healthy and happy in a relationship that involves intimacy of that kind requires understanding yourself and the other person, knowing your wants and needs, and communicating kindly with your partner. This is very Zen.

Understanding where common problems can arise in a sexual relationship is important in this discussion. Fear, guilt, moral differences, and common taboos can all lead to problems in an intimate relationship, but it can also be understood or worked through. Understand that just like anything else, sex is not a bad or good thing, by itself. Only the actions of the participants can give it that meaning.

Another aspect that can cause friction in a relationship of this kind is when sex is the only thing the relationship is based on. It is common for a couple to come together through mutual attraction and passion without having any knowledge or understanding of their partner. Remember, sex is not essential for a strong relationship, even a romantic one. It is a secondary aspect that should not come first if the goal is a long and healthy union.

Allow your loving relationship to grow. The sexual aspect should form naturally in the context of that love to create a stronger relationship. Starting with sex may mean that there is nothing to fall back on when the passion is not there. This could result in other things taking precedence in a couple's life.

You should also remember that Zen has no tolerance for harming other people, including sexual acts. Do not do anything to your partner that they do not want and make sure to stop if they want you to, even if they previously consented to have sex. Do not coerce people into having sex with you through force, guilt, or deceit. Do not cheat on your partner. It is much better to discuss problems rationally and decide if it is time to separate as a couple than to lie and cheat. Understand your partner's needs and do your best to meet them. If you do not do your best to understand your partner, then you are denying their humanity and individuality.

Zen is a practice of growing to understand and love yourself as well as those around you. Applying this practice to your most intimate relationships will make it a happier and longer-lasting partnership. Use the teachings of Zen to work through problems, keep your patience when times are hard, continue working on yourself, and understand the needs of the relationship.

<u>Chapter 4: Applying Zen to Your Work</u>

If you were to ask a random number of people if their job was stressful, most of them would probably say yes. You might have a stressful job that you hate, but even well-loved jobs will still have rough days. This chapter is for helping you get through those stressful and infuriating times at work to find peace with your job through Zen practices.

Five ways to practice Zen at work

- *Daily habits*

Forming daily habits might seem like a simple thing, maybe even too simple. It's really that easy though. Forming good work habits will help you manage your time, stress levels, and feel better while working. Start by identifying your bad work habits, good work habits, and the habits you would like to form.

Some examples of good Zen-focused work habits are focusing your efforts on helping others, make sure you are eating, drinking, and breathing well, prioritize tasks to get the most important ones out of the way first, take time off (really off, don't check emails off the clock!), improve posture whether you're standing or working at a desk, practicing mindful meditation, and taking breaks when needed.

Take some or all of these habits into your daily routine or make some of your own at work and observe how much better you will feel at the end of the day. Your quality of work will increase, and you will become more efficient once you implement some simple changes to your habits.

- ***Be present at the moment***

We have covered being more present in the here and now earlier in this book, but it deserves to be mentioned again now that we're talking about work. It is a hard thing for some people to do while working, but it can help make you happier every single day. Most people tie their happiness at work with success, but success does not equal happiness. When will you be successful enough to be happy? When will you stop striving for the next goal in line while promising yourself you'll be happy when it's complete? Will you even be happy then anyways? Probably not.

A good example is someone working towards a promotion. Yes, the promotion might come with a raise and benefits, and that would make anyone happy. But if this person is too caught up in their goal, they might miss another job opportunity, their family activities, or lose interest in their hobbies. That would mean that they are missing out on the happiness they could have felt in pursuit of the elusive happiness that might never come.

No one can truly enjoy their life if their happiness depends on fulfilling certain conditions. One could say you will only end up missing the forest by focusing on the trees. Take time to enjoy the simple things in life. Yes, this includes work. Give each day your full attention and enjoy the little things. Do not deprive yourself of happiness by comparing yourself to someone more successful.

- ***Let go***

Not everything will run smoothly, fairly, logically, or even successfully. For a job, this is especially true. The sooner you can accept it and let the bad things go, the sooner you can focus on moving on to the next step. You should not be holding on to the stress from bad projects, annoying coworkers, ruthless bosses, or rude customers.

Recognize that a lot of the stress you get from work is not from work itself, but from your desire for things to be different. Remember, Zen teaches us that suffering is born from desire. To desire things that do not happen makes you unhappy and stressed out. If you accept that you cannot always change an outcome, you can let the results go. Once you understand that it's not what happened that is making you upset, but your reaction to it, you can change that reaction for the better.

Imagine driving home from work. You might expect that you get back easily as usual, then when you get a flat tire or run into unexpected road construction you end up frustrated. If only you let go of the expectation of a simple drive back from the beginning, then you would not have accrued the extra stress.

Learning to let go, a process of accepting Zen into your life and workplace, will not likely be instant and will take time and practice. Start with little things and eventually your entire day will be filled with Zen.

- *Do not overdo it*

Not overdoing it at work might be hard for some people. A lot of jobs put emphasis on willpower, pushing through, and working until you drop as good traits for employees to have. This is unfortunate, but there are some things you can to stop yourself from overworking, even in the most demanding jobs.

People have a limited amount of energy in a day, and once you run out, there won't be enough to sustain your desire to keep working. Employers should understand this, but not all of them do. Regardless, both at a job or you're when working for yourself, try not to use up all of your energy all at once.

A lot of this comes down to avoiding what wears you out. You wouldn't have junk food in your house if you're on a diet, right? This is the same concept. Avoid grabbing extra work or talking to stressful coworkers if possible. Use techniques like listening to music or eating snacks on a break to keep your willpower and happiness up.

Another part is not taking pride in being busy. Don't be the kind of person that is answering emails and phone calls every single hour of the day, staying late all the time, or refusing to take days off. All that does is burn you out, and you end up stressed. You are only destroying your potential to do more. This is not Zen either since you should be putting your full attention into every task. You cannot do that if you're needlessly tired.

- ### *Avoid negativity and quick judgment*

As discussed earlier in this book, refraining from quick judgment and the negativity it causes is good Zen advice. Avoid working yourself up over the actions of others. Everyone has their own life and reasons for acting. Resist the urge to give into negativity and fan the fire at the workplace when something goes wrong. Stop the momentum of negative thoughts, and don't judge the actions of the people around you until you know the entire story.

Make an effort to understand the motivations of other people. Their actions might have been justified from their point of view. Noticing this will allow you to bring a positive attitude to a discussion as you try solving the problem. Follow the advice in the previous chapter for dealing with relationships from a Zen-centered perspective when working with other people.

How to become a Zen manager

If you are a manager, run a team, own a business, or just want to someday, there is some special

Zen advice for you. Being in charge of the actions of other people is an important position that should not be taken lightly. You should be going about your job with kindness and an open mind as instructed by the Zen teachings.

The main point is to act with no preconceptions of what will happen. Keep yourself open, do not judge without knowledge, and remain fully present at the moment.

It is also a Zen practice to help others in everything they do. That means you should put your own needs behind those of the people who look to you for instruction. As a manager, you should be operating with the seriousness of a *Bodhisattva* in the sense that everything you do on the job is meant to improve the efficiency of the workplace and aid the workers.

A manager should be considerate towards their subordinates. There are many ways this can be done. However, most people who work as a manager would rather refuse a lot of the people they work with. The salary you give should be enough to provide enough for necessities and comfort, the materials for completing the work should be safe and functioning, the employees should be trained properly and given chances for advancement and autonomy, and rewards and credit should be given when due.

Providing these things will empower employees. Empowered employees will work harder, be more efficient, and be happier while working. The world outside the job will be better as well. When employees are paid enough, burdens are removed from their families, and they become patrons of other businesses in the area.

Besides your subordinates, you should also support your coworkers and bosses. Supporting your subordinates means a better work environment, and you will likely earn their support in turn. Supporting people above you means you will be pulled up with them when they do well. It is a mistake to buy into the 'dog-eat-dog' mentality that is common at workplaces. Loving your fellow human beings by supporting those that you work with will not lead you astray. Bring out the best in others, and they will bring out the best in you.

That being said, what happens if you cannot be kind to someone? What if they broke a rule, hurt a coworker, or stole from the company? You cannot keep them employed, which is obviously not the kind thing to do. Except that it is. By keeping someone who is harming the environment you have worked so hard, you will be ruining the peaceful workplace you built. This is where in Zen, compassion, and wisdom are in contrast with one another. To maintain your Zen, you must find the balance of these two ideals. In that situation, it would mean letting go of that troublesome employee to maintain your ideal of a kind and peaceful work environment for the rest of the employees. Use your knowledge to deal with each new situation.

Overall, as a manager, you must strive to embody the teachings of Zen the most. You will not be a successful leader if you do not understand yourself and have not bothered understanding others. Follow what the 'Eightfold Path' teaches us in every action you make, and the correct path will be shown to you.

Whether you're working for a business or have your own venture, maintain a Zen-centered perspective will help you keep peace and remain stress-free as much as possible. You should learn not to rely on external factors for your emotional well-being. Instead, you must keep yourself steady in the face of all circumstances. Remember to look for happiness now, not later, and avoid making preemptive judgments. By following the advice in this chapter, you will be able to improve your daily work as well as advance your long-term career.

Chapter 5: Applying Zen to Your Finances

To understand how you can apply Zen in managing your finances, you need to learn about the relationship between Buddhism and money. It is traditionally considered bad karma for Buddhist monks to handle money. This is unrealistic for the average person in today's world though. The reasoning for this rule lies within the history of monastic traditions where money was not an essential thing. Monasteries around the world still practice not handling money, but it is rarely, if ever, seen outside of those confined spaces.

 The idea is that money cannot grant you happiness but will instead bring you away from understanding. Money is thought to inherently cause more greed, selfishness, and cruelty in people. This could be quite true. The more wealth a person accumulates, the less they see their fellow human beings as equals. They will become more autonomous and as such, have less accountability to other people. Just look at how the beautiful lawns in 'elite' neighborhoods are kept pristine even in times of drought. All of this is done at the expense of the other people who depend on the watershed.

To live in a more Zen way regarding money, you do not have to give it up or voluntarily live in poverty. However, it is generally taught that everyone should live within their means without seeking extreme wealth. Remember, money is a tool with no good or bad meaning until we give it meaning. If you do good things with your money, then it is good, and vice versa. Although you should avoid falling into the trap of thinking that money can solve all your problems.

Regardless, you have to handle money to survive in today's society. This will have effects on your life that you cannot control, but there are ways you can achieve a balance of Zen while doing so. Below are five ways that can help you improve your financial situation with Zen by spending less and saving more.

Five methods for improving your finances with Zen

- *Resist impulsive spending*

Impulsivity does not have a place in Zen. Desiring things leads to suffering and unhappiness. The cure for this is to become self-aware. If you see something you want and cannot have, you become unhappy but to get rid of this feeling you just have to understand why you want the thing. Make sure that it is a 'need' and not a 'want' before purchasing. If you analyze why you want to buy something, you may discover that it is not as necessary as you previously thought.

To understand why you have an impulse to spend money, keep a log or look at your bank records to see where, when, and how much you spend at various places. Do you have a long list of small purchases throughout the day? If the answer is yes, you may be impulsively buying things.

Think about how many times you ate out at a restaurant for lunch or dinner, bought new clothes you didn't even need, or even paid for a new game or application on your phone. All of those little purchases add up. Maybe you needed to eat out because you forgot to pack lunch once. In that case, it's alright. What's important is you understood that was a need. The times you decided to go out with your friends or coworkers to lunch, even though you already brought something from home, is what you would classify as a 'want.'

Spending a little on your wants is not a bad thing. You cannot remove yourself from all of your hobbies, pastimes, or entertainment of course. However, you must learn to accept that those are not essential purchases so that you will be more careful in making your choices.

Do you have problems keeping your credit card paid off? This is a great first step to getting out of minor debt. Maybe choosing to buy fewer things per month will help, even if it's just one less cup of coffee or bag of chips. Not only will you be spending less money, but you can now put the savings towards the debt or more important things like bills.

- ***Focus on essentials***

Focusing on essentials is related to reducing your impulsive spending. By learning to focus on what you need, you can break free from the vicious cycle of earning less and spending more. Get rid of the idea that the things you buy or can afford to buy are a reflection of your personality. If you are well off, understand that it does not matter if you have the most expensive and latest possessions. If you are not well off, understand that it does not matter if you cannot buy items from known brands. These things do not weigh your morals or how good of a person you can be.

Learn to focus on bare essentials. Purchasing

something should fulfill a need, not a want, as explained above. A good example is, even if you can afford it, do you really need more than one or two large televisions in your home? Do you really need to buy the third one even if it is on sale? If you have the money for a new television, then you would have the money for other, more fulfilling prospects like going on a vacation with your family, donating to charity, or setting it aside for your savings.

Speaking of lesser expenses, do you need a brand name option every time you have to replace something in your house? Using less expensive options will make using the brand name options more of a special occasion or luxury. Perhaps you may even discover that spending more was pointless because the cheaper item was just as good.

Learn to recognize these patterns. If you decide brand name items or a new television are necessities, then it may be worth it to buy them. However, you should be able to decide whether they are or not. Understand your reasons for wanting things versus needing things.

- *Be truthful about your money*

Being truthful with your money starts with being truthful with yourself. Remember that lying is not accepted within the tenets of the Zen philosophy. Learn to be honest with yourself about how much you can afford and stick to it. You cannot delude yourself into buying more than you can if you really can't afford it. There are, of course, circumstances where even essentials might be more than what your budget can afford, but this is for the times when you want something, but it would mean you would have to give up the need to buy it. Do not do this.

Make a budget and work on understanding it completely. Understand where you spend, why, and how much. Notice patterns and subtract essential bills like rent or mortgage, electric, transportation, food, and water before setting aside money for entertainment and luxuries. This is only a basic instruction on how you can budget your money. There is more information about budgeting later in this chapter and if this seems like something that will help you, be sure to look further into it.

Another way to be truthful with your money is to talk about it with your partner, family, or roommates. Money can lead to extreme stress on relationships. Talking about it with other people can help you work together on budgeting to reduce stress. Talking about money with your partner will also help you plan for your future together. Review your finances with someone every few weeks at least.

Also, avoid bragging about your spending, especially in public. Avoid sharing too much about the successes of your business, how much you gave to charity, or personal gains on a public forum. There really is no need to do so and talking about yourself too much can lead to unexpected problems. Show your success subtly and let your true self, removed from your attachment to money, be revealed to the world instead.

The opposite is true as well. Avoid complaining about money problems in public for similar reasons. Money should have no bearing on your true self.

- *Create routine spending habits*

Creating good habits is a very Zen-oriented concept, and it can be easily applied to your financial decisions. Keep good records, pay your bills as soon as you can, and even make your payments automatic if possible. All of these are relatively simple habits that will help you immensely in the long term.

Keeping your records in order will help you understand your spending habits and your taxes since you will be a more informed spender. Plus, keeping good records means you can find ways to save on your taxes. The donations, business spending, and medical expenses are common tax deductions that can save you money.

Paying your bills, as soon as they come in, is one way to keep your spending organized. Write a check or pay online the moment the bill arrives in the mail. Do not put it off because you can lose the bill or even forget to pay it. Late charges or getting services turned off are not ideal situations while trying to save money and will only give you more stress.

If you are able, making them automatic will help with this process, but it will require that you always have money in your account to cover them. Avoid automatic payments if you can't afford them since overdraft charges can ruin your budget.

- *Create a budget*

Create a budget, also known as a monthly spending plan that outlines your limits for expenses.

Budgeting might be one of the best tools available for managing your finances and learning to save money. There is a reason it is praised in so many financial help books and classes. As you probably know, a budget is an outline of expenses. You should organize it in a way that makes sense for you. You should also budget both monthly and yearly. Holidays, birthdays, vacations, and unexpected expenses can be easily budgeted in a year than on a month-to-month basis. Remember, a budget should not trap you into rigid spending, but rather, it should free your mind from worrying if you can afford something or not.

After creating a budget, it is important to monitor it. Review it every week or two to maintain control. Take time to regularly balance your checkbook, monitor automatic payments, check your debt/s, and review your savings. Remember to do this with your partner, if you have one.

A good tip for budgeting is to keep your finances simple. Limit the number of accounts and credit cards as much as possible. We suggest only maintain a maximum of one bank and one credit card. Simplify your investment accounts as well.

This chapter is meant to be a guide for you to begin using Zen to manage your finances. None of these tips for managing your financial situation are set in stone. Sometimes, budgets just cannot be kept because of unforeseen circumstances and living from paycheck to paycheck makes it difficult to keep payments up to date. All of that is okay. Just remember to keep a positive and peaceful mindset when dealing with your finances along with the trouble it entails.

Chapter 6: The Benefits of Zen on Health and Happiness

Since you made it this far in the book, you probably have a good idea of how Zen can improve your happiness and what some of the health benefits of Zen are. This chapter will be covering those topics in more detail, starting with what the health benefits of practicing meditation are, followed by how meditation works on the body, and we will end with how you can make yourself more happy by embodying a Zen-oriented lifestyle.

Zen and health

The main benefit to your health will come from meditation. Meditation helps the spiritual, mental, and physical well-being of people who practice it regularly. This book has covered how meditation helps improve mindfulness and understanding, and how it can help you move toward a more peaceful mind free from distractions.

Better sleep

Sleep is important for repairing your body and

keeping everything in working order. Meditating regularly and keeping a Zen-inspired outlook throughout the rest of your day will help you sleep more soundly. You will have fewer things to burden your mind, and your body will relax easier. Getting good, consistent sleep will also have positive benefits on your immune system and allow you to fight off common ailments easier.

Improves posture

Good posture helps strength, flexibility, agility, keeps your spine healthy, and prevents muscle strain. Additionally, you will look better and stand taller with good posture. Meditating correctly forces you to sit with good posture. After some practice, your posture will gradually improve. Maintaining good posture throughout your life will help you stay fit and flexible as you age, and avoid injuries to the knees, hips, and back.

Reduces body pain

Besides removing pain associated with weakness and muscle strain because of bad posture, you might also see a reduction in other pains as well. Meditation can help people reduce their pain sensitivity by teaching us to cope better by not dwelling on the pain itself.

Mindfulness has been lauded as a technique for reducing pain and pain's effects on the mind and body for hundreds of years. It might not be an alternative for other pain-relieving treatments, but it could be worth trying if the pain you feel is starting to have drastic effects on your quality of life.

Lowers blood pressure and improves blood flow

While meditating, you sit still and focus on calming yourself. This has the natural effect of lowering your heart rate and breathing rate and improving your blood circulation. This has numerous health benefits such as making sure you have more energy and experience less pain throughout the day.

Reduce stress

Reducing stress and lowering your anxiety level are probably the main health benefits of meditation and having a Zen lifestyle. Lowering your stress level will not only make you happier but much healthier as well. You will have more energy to focus on important things and be less susceptible to sickness. Stress can even cause most of the issues discussed above.

Why it works

Stress-related health problems are an epidemic in the modern world. They even make up as much as eighty percent of the population that pay the doctor a visit. This alone is a very good reason why we should learn about what stress is and how to lessen its effects on the body. Even though stress reduction has been proven to be important for health, not very many medical professionals are equipped to deal with it. Fortunately, you can help yourself by practicing meditation or something similar, like yoga.

 Meditation has been shown to lower stress by improving your relaxation response and lowering your stress-inducing hormones. Stress is a reaction that will quicken your heart rate and breathing rate and raise your blood pressure. On top of that, an excessive quantity of stress-inducing hormones in your body will negatively affect your organs, brain functions, and your immune system.

 Stress has even been linked to the development

of more serious problems such as headaches, migraines, mental health issues like depression, and even heart disease can be caused by stress. Because of the fact that stress is unavoidable in everyday life, striving to reduce your stress, even if it's only by a small margin, should be a priority. Meditation has been proven to help by fostering a relaxed state of being where your stress response can no longer react.

You have probably learned about your stress response at some point by hearing it called a 'fight-or-flight response' or an 'adrenaline rush.' This is an important function of your body, but it can become a burden if you experience it too often. It's more than just a faster heart rate. Hormones are released, your nerves are put on high alert, you sweat more, breath quicker, your immune system is activated, your blood pressure rises, and less important body functions start to shut down.

This means that your digestion and the repair of body tissue stops. Your immune system will be too overworked to function when it needs to, and your mood will fluctuate violently because of the extra hormones in your system. You may become numb to stimuli like excitement or joy because your mind is being overstimulated by stress. Having chronic stress could even mean that your response kicks in more often and is slower to turn off.

59

It might seem like all of that is too much for meditation and a Zen lifestyle to handle, however, you will be surprised by how helpful it can really be. Recent research has led to the understanding that purposefully enacting your relaxation response regularly can reduce the effects that stress has on the body. It will help your body turn off the stress response and reverse some of the negative effects it has.

The relaxation response is basically the opposite of the previously mentioned fight-or-flight response. It is defined as your body's ability to release hormones that negates the stress response and signals your muscles to relax and stimulates the increase of blood flow. By meditating, you will learn how to turn on the relaxation response and thus, turn off the stress response, returning your body to a healthy, stress-free status.

Health problems linked to stress

Below is a list of health problems that have been linked to stress. Stress can either contribute to or make them worse. Practicing mindful meditation has been shown to help reduce and reverse symptoms of many of the problems listed below and more.

- Anxiety
- Arthritis
- Constipation
- Depression
- Diabetes
- Headaches
- Heart problems
- Heartburn
- High blood pressure
- Infectious diseases (such as a cold)
- Insomnia
- Irritable bowel syndrome
- Pain
- Parkinson's disease
- Side effects of cancer and cancer treatments
- Slow wound healing
- Ulcers

Meditation, as well as practices like acupuncture, massage, visualization, prayer, breathing techniques, yoga, *tai chi*, or *qi gong,* can all help reduce your stress by activating the relaxation response. Meditation is the most common method of inducing the relaxation response and can be easily learned by everyone. Learning how to meditate and embody a Zen-oriented outlook will have positive benefits for your health, whether you are currently suffering from ailments, or if you just want to prevent any possible health problems from occurring.

Zen and happiness

As you have learned in this book, Zen teaches us that suffering is born from desire. So, to achieve happiness, you must understand and work to get rid of your desires. Everyone is looking for happiness, and it is the main force behind most human actions, which makes it a key point in being human. Getting over desires is an important step to embodying Zen and gaining the benefits it offers.

First, you need to understand happiness from a Zen-oriented perspective. Happiness in Zen is not something you should be looking for. Instead, it comes naturally without effort. Zen teaches us that we should be mindful, helpful, and understanding when it comes to yourself and others. It also teaches that we must always act with the intention to do good and that by successfully doing so, happiness will come to you unabated.

Individualistic desires get in the way of the Zen philosophy. Having wants inevitably leads to disappointment, frustration, and anger if they are not fulfilled. Though, achieving these wants do not always lead to the feelings we expected. It becomes a cycle of never being happy enough, and we always end up searching for more.

It just is not possible to remain happy with a never-ending stream of desires holding you back. Any happiness you gain from this method will be temporary and unfulfilling. It is simply the result of the reward center of your brain being triggered when something you want comes to fruition, it is not long-term happiness.

When we say 'short-term happiness' we refer to things like good food, new possessions, money, or good news. They make you feel secure, but not for long. These things are not bad on their own, and you do not have to stop eating or being glad when something good happens. It just means that you should accept that things will never bring you true, life-long happiness. You should not try to suppress your desires but learn from them and suppress your *attachment* to them.

So, what do you do for long-term happiness? Most of the feelings of satisfaction and happiness you have when you get something you want are the result of subconscious thought processes. Long-term thinking meanwhile, is a result of conscious thought processes. This means that you have to become aware of your needs, wants, thought processes, and your place in the world.

Zen is the perfect way to learn more about long-lasting and fulfilling happiness. Mindful meditation allows you to move past the simple parts of your thoughts and think bigger. Once you have moved past your desires, you can follow the 'Eightfold Paths' to achieving things that provide more than instant, quick-to-dissipate satisfaction.

As a reminder, here are the 'Eightfold Paths' and how to follow them:

- ***Right view***

  Become aware of the actions you take, the actions of others, and the motivations behind them and understand that nothing is permanent, including your idea of 'self.'

- ***Right Intention***

  Become aware of your feelings of desire, judgment, and anger and resist acting on them. Be sure to only act if your intentions are motivated by doing good things for others, not just yourself.

- *Right speech*

  Keep in mind that words can harm other people, which is why you need to be careful with what you say. Do not lie, spread deceit, or speak harshly. Speak only if you have something nice to say or contribute.

- *Right action*

  Do not harm people, animals, or your surroundings. This includes murder, theft, and molestation above all else.

- *Right livelihood*

  This path means living honestly by doing a job that will help others. Do not do something just to get rich or with the intention of harming. Avoid dealing with weapons, meat production, alcohol, or drugs and do not engage in a profession in which the goals are contrary to right speech and right action.

- *Right effort*

  Apply effort in making the correct actions by not doing something that can hurt others and actively doing good things whenever possible.

- *Right mindfulness*

  This refers to observing and understanding yourself to focus on the here and now. This also refers to refraining from making a quick judgment or making incorrect interpretations.

- *Right concentration*

  This refers to meditation and achieving a greater level of understanding through a focused mind.

True feelings of happiness will be achieved naturally through these steps. Being kind and having the right intentions in life will reward you. If you do good things, it will come back to you. This concept is commonly called the 'law of attraction,' or better known as *karma*. Whatever you send out into the universe, you shall receive back. So, send out happiness if your goal is happiness. It might sound counter-intuitive, but by not focusing on your own happiness, you eventually reach the true happiness found only in the Zen way of life.

<u>Conclusion</u>

Thank you for making it through to the end of *Zen for Beginners: Your Guide to Achieving Happiness and Finding Inner Peace with Zen in Your Everyday Life*, let's hope it was informative and that it provided you with all of the tools you need to achieve your goals whatever they may be.

Hopefully, by reading this book, you have gained the knowledge and tools to start practicing Zen. This book has given you an introduction to the history and practices in the Zen philosophy, an understanding on how to practice Zen in your everyday life, how to apply Zen to your relationships, work, and finances, as well as how it can benefit your health and happiness.

As you now know, anyone can apply Zen to their lifestyle regardless of their beliefs, social status, or health. Practicing a Zen lifestyle will help you in a multitude of ways, probably even more than what has been discussed in this book. You will reduce your stress, improve your relationships, and learn some new things about yourself in the process.

The next step is to begin your journey towards embodying Zen in your everyday life through practice and meditation. The changes you will make in your life might even be noticeable to others. If this book has helped you change your life for the better, do not be shy about sharing with other people how the philosophy of Zen has helped you.

Finally, if you found this book useful in any way, a review on Amazon is always appreciated!

Other Books By The Author

Printed in Poland
by Amazon Fulfillment
Poland Sp. z o.o., Wrocław

58556947R00040